Wind and the Night Monsters

Wind and the Night Monsters

Stories in Verse from Montana

By Carol Hample

Printed in the United States of America

Library of Congress Catalog Card Number: 93-91615
ISBN 1-56044-235-2

Text illustrations by Andrea Art
Cover illustration by Eric Heidle

Published by Carol Hample,
P.O. Box 7177, Bozeman, Montana 59771-7177
in cooperation with SkyHouse Publishers,
an imprint of Falcon Press Publishing Co., Inc.,
Helena, Montana.

Design, typesetting, and other prepress work
by Falcon Graphics, Helena, Montana.

To Dad,
who taught me to love poetry

Contents

Contents
(continued)

Preface: Poetry on Poetry

It's an art every time to create a good rhyme
From the words that our language provides.
They must sound just the same to lay claim to that fame,
And have just the right meaning besides.

For example, a word may appear as it's heard,
Or may not, as in words such as *push*.
If you say it like *rush*, you will probably blush,
Since it should be pronounced as in *bush*.

And your problems will mount with the syllable count,
Unless accented right at the end,
Because *vertex* and *vortex* don't both rhyme with *cortex*,
But *misapprehend* matches *bend*.

Creativity drag is another big snag,
Because forcing a rhyme really shows.
If I patiently wait for my mind to create,
Then the poetry naturally flows.

And the rhythm, of course, is a powerful force
In the overall flow of the verse.
If the meter is wrong for the sonnet or song,
Then it makes it progressively worse.

If the rhythm and rhyme are exact every time,
And the meter is chosen okay,
Then the work has potential with one last essential—
It has to have something to say.

Dad's Early Years

My father has always told me colorful stories of his adventures pushing the envelope of life. Since I could never remember the details or just how he understated and abbreviated without losing the full impact, he began obliging me by writing down his stories to me in letters.

Of course, one story leads to another, as you may discover in your own mind as you read about Dad's adventures.

Model T's had a hand throttle so between holding on & operating the throttle I can't wipe the tears or blood away so can't see & can't stop & can't steer going up steep rocky hill. Poor Johnny in back trying to hold barrel full of water with us going over rocks & jackknifing all over the hill

My First Memory

The first thing that I can remember was when
I was only a small boy of three.
They were building the courthouse in Stanford and I
was inspecting the job for them, free.

It was just about then that I saw the big house,
N. B. Matthews' big house, moving by.
Perry Hunt was transporting the structure to Stanford
from where it had been in Lehigh.

With a pair of steam tractors in tandem he pulled it,
their engines chug-chugging away,
With the wheels made of steel that were under the house
leaving ruts in the road all the way.

But the reason it sticks in my mind to this day,
even though I was then only three,
Was because on that day in the middle of town,
Perry Hunt blew the whistle at me!

A Walk in the Dark

I still remember well one night
some fifty years ago,
When Johnny Hardenbrook and I
were boys of twelve or so.
The night was black as pitch with heavy
clouds, but fairly still,
And warm enough to walk to Sun Creek
Ranch across the hill.

The higher in the clouds we got,
the darker it became.
No stars, no light to see a thing,
it all looked just the same.
Our flashlight wasn't very good,
but probably enough.
We only had to use it when
the going got too rough.

We knew where we were going, never
worried in the least.
A fence would stop us to the west,
another to the east.
We helped to build those fences, couldn't
miss them if we tried.
So we just headed up the hill
and down the other side.

We walked along while telling lies
as only boys know how,
When suddenly I blindly hit
the broadside of a cow!
It scared the hell right out of me,
that warm and hairy thing.
I didn't know just what I had,
so dark and everything.

When Johnny turned the light on,
there she was, a nice old cow.
She didn't want to move, and she
was sleepy anyhow.
She didn't even then, I hadn't
shocked her in the least.
We had to walk around her, that old
warm and hairy beast.

Spring Water

On the Hardenbrook ranch, where we worked our own pace,
Was a pretty good spring on the way to Duane's place.
We had made a small pool so the water could flow
Through a small one-inch pipe to the trough down below.

There was plenty of water, a little stream flowing,
And around everything there were willow trees growing.
We were pretty inventive those days on the ranch,
And so somebody hung a glass jar on a branch.
That way, while your horse got a drink from the trough,
You could drink from the pipe and not even get off!

One day after drinking my fill from the spout,
With the water flow down, and just trickling out,
I decided to see what the problem could be.
There was plenty of water, it seemed like to me.

So I checked to see what could be plugging the pipe,
And I found a dead woodchuck that smelled pretty ripe.
It had been a while, too, since the critter had died,
For the hair was just starting to slip from the hide.
No, I didn't get sick like today people would,
And I thought that spring water was pretty darn good!

Old Socks

A little black mare, kinda spooky but tame,
Had socks on all fours, and so Socks was her name.
She and I had been out on the trail all day,
Doing what, I've forgotten, but earning our pay.
We were both pretty tired and could use a drink soon,
So we headed for home in the late afternoon.

She was taking one step at a time as she went
With her nose in the dust and her energy spent.
I was half asleep, too, and my backside was worn,
So to rest it, I hooked my leg over the horn.
Then I pulled my hat down so it covered my eyes,
Though I knew to be out of control wasn't wise.

When suddenly I'm in the dust on my knee
With a rattlesnake coiled and staring at me!
I took four hops backwards with no place to hide,
For it seems that Old Socks was ten feet to one side.
Even though we were tired on that hot summer day,
We were both wide awake for the rest of the way.

The Bull Story

In the summer the cattle could range quite a ways
Up the dry fork of Belt Creek to lazily graze.
There were cow-and-calf pairs and two bulls that would roam
Until fall when the first winter storm brought them home.

Well, one year they appeared when we got our first snow.
All the cows had returned, but the bulls didn't show,
So we waited two weeks for the next winter storm.
Now, those bulls were expensive! And tempers got warm.

When they still didn't show, we decided to go
To the forest to get them before too much snow.
It was ten or twelve miles across country by horse,
And a pretty long day, with no lunches, of course.

It was warm in the sun and a pretty nice day,
And we found the two bulls by their tracks right away.
But they went in the jack pines and wouldn't come out.
They decided to stay the whole winter, no doubt.

Now the horses hung back, and we knew how they felt,
For the snow on the branches had started to melt.
But with hats over faces we headed on in,
And in just twenty feet we were soaked to the skin.

And around and around in that forested shower
We chased those damn bulls for at least half an hour.
We were madder than hell and about to explode!
And then finally we got them back out on the road.

With a bull whip we galloped them maybe a mile,
And then slowed to a walk again after a while.
It got darker and colder the further we went,
And we both were still wet with our energy spent.

'Till we came to the base of the Blankenship Hill
And decided to stop there to ward off the chill.
In an old mining cabin the floor boards were drier
Than anything else, so we built a good fire.

Since the bulls had grown fat, they were worn out for sure,
And the horses were pooped, so they stood where they were.
Well we finally warmed up, and we started to ride
Over Blankenship Hill and then down the far side.

And by pounding the bulls on the butt all the way,
We got home about midnight, a pretty long day.
We were hungry and tired, as I can recall,
But those two truant bulls were more tired than us all!

The Steering Wheel

I was often in trouble and never got bored
In the days I was driving my Model T Ford.
It was simple to operate, easy to fix,
If you knew how it worked and a couple of tricks.

It had brakes and reverse and a low and high gear,
But you had to push hard with your foot, that was clear.
And the steering wheel I had replaced on my T,
For the Model A version was larger, you see.

It was thicker though, too, with no room for the nut,
But if there was a problem, I didn't know what.
It was keyed so the wheel wouldn't slip, anyway,
And the steering was easy. I liked it that way.

My friend Johnny and I often worked as a team.
If we didn't have chores, we would cook up some scheme.
We were hauling a barrel of water one day
Up a pretty steep hill for the T, I would say.

Now the barrel was topless, so Johnny was riding
In back to prevent that old barrel from sliding.
The steep part was rocky, the going was rough,
But we're under control, and it wasn't so tough.

I push hard on the pedal to keep it in gear,
And to brace I pull up on the wheel as I steer.
Well, it came off and hit me smack dab on the nose,
But that smacking was only the start of my woes.

Well, I had to grab something to keep pushing down,
For the brakes wouldn't hold, though I felt like a clown.
With one hand on the throttle and one holding on,
And I can't wipe my face, and my dignity gone,

With the blood and the tears I can't see and can't steer
And can't stop on that slope—oh, my plight was severe!
And poor Johnny in back as we jerked up the hill
Was still holding the barrel so it wouldn't spill.

After lurching and jerking our way to the top,
Where the brakes finally held and we came to a stop,
We were under control and were glad we had fought 'er,
But had to go back down the hill for more water.

Basil Skelton

A few of us were hunting from
        a cabin, I recall,
The one on old Doc Williams' place,
        one year in early fall.
One night it snowed about a foot
        of wet and heavy snow,
So we decided then the Model A
        would have to go.

The road was up the hill from where
        we'd left the Model A,
So in the snow we chained 'er up,
        which should have worked okay.
But still we couldn't make it,
        for the snow was pretty deep,
So all of us got out to push,
        and it was fairly steep.

The driver gave her hell and must
        have had a wild ride,
And Basil Skelton I remember
        pushing on the side.
His footing slipped and down he went,
        and though we saw him fall,
We didn't stop and ran right over Basil,
        chains and all.

He lay there on his face in heavy snow,
        and dead no doubt,
So when we made it to the road,
        we went to check him out.
But he was up and raising hell,
        and we could see the track.
It started on his butt and angled
        right across his back.

Undressing him, we saw the only
        damage we had done
Was narrow marks at four inch spaces
        where the chain had run.
It didn't break the skin, but it was
        tender to the touch,
But even so it didn't slow
        the hunting very much...

The Flat Tire

It was during the thirties when I was in school,
And my Model T Ford worked okay as a rule,
But one day Fatty Aamold was going with me
To haul ashes away to the dump with the T.

Now the tires were thin and would often go flat,
But we knew what to do and could remedy that.
Because one guy could easily lift up one end,
So a block could be placed underneath by his friend.

But that day with a load, and a flat on the rear,
It was really too heavy to lift, that was clear.
So I pulled out a pole from a jack fence nearby,
And I shoved it up under, and lifted 'er high.

But as Fatty was under there setting the block,
The pole broke, and down came the T like a rock!
Poor old Fatty was six inches shorter and bruised,
And I laughed at his plight, but he wasn't amused.

Mom's Early Years

I thoroughly enjoy listening to people's stories. Each story reveals a little bit more about the teller, not just from the tale but also through the telling. Dad's early stories draw a picture not only of life in the early 1930s in Montana, but also of him as a young man, of his perceptions of what happened around him. As Mom reminisces about the same time and place, the person that is Mom begins to appear.

She remembers her early years, not so much in the form of escapades, but rather as the details of daily life. Mom's stories evoke a poignancy felt by many growing up during the Depression in Montana.

The Wash Tub

When I was five, or maybe four,
And youngest of us all,
And we were living on the ranch,
The first thing I recall

Was on a summer Saturday
And Mom had filled the tub
And set it in the sun to heat
So all of us could scrub.

Our cousins had come down to play,
And we were having fun,
And then they made me take my bath
In front of everyone!

I don't know how my sisters bathed,
Or what the others did.
I just remember I was one
Embarrassed little kid!

Growing Up In Montana

When I was a kid
And we lived where we did
    On a ranch about two miles from town,
Then I guess you could say
We were poor, in a way,
    With our revenue being way down.

But we lived like our peers
For at least seven years—
    Like forever it seemed to me then.
Because I was just three
When we moved there, you see,
    And had learned quite a bit by age ten.

We were clean and well-fed,
As we frequently said,
    But to grow all our food was a chore.
We made everything there,
Because money was rare,
    And we couldn't just run to the store.

We had turkeys and chickens,
Who squawked like the dickens
    When Dad went to chop off their head.
And we'd usually keep
A few pigs and some sheep
    To have pork chops or mutton instead.

We had milk cows, of course,
Because they were the source
    Of our milk and our butter and cream.
And quite early we learned
How the butter was churned,
    And drank warm foamy milk like a dream.

But we kept the milk cold
To be bottled and sold,
        And my sister and I helped deliver.
And we'd give away some
When the gypsies would come.
        Then the bottles we'd find by the river.

In the summer we played
With our dolls in the shade
        In the ice house where it was so nice.
It was layered with straw
So the blocks wouldn't thaw,
        And we'd chip it and eat the cold ice.

But the kitchen was warm
In a cold winter storm
        Where the wood-and-coal range was our heat.
When we came home from school
And our bottoms were cool,
        Then the reservoir made a good seat.

And the reservoir water
Was usually hotter
        On Saturday night for the tub.
For we wouldn't be seen
Unless perfectly clean
        While in Sunday school. That was the rub.

As I sit here like this,
And retell, reminisce,
        I see good times as well as the bad,
And along with the sorrow
And hope for tomorrow,
        The love and the joy that we had!

Drought

In the spring we had hopefully planted our seeds,
And had tended them lovingly, keeping out weeds,
        As we waited, we waited, for rain.
There was plenty of sunshine and long growing days,
And the shimmer of summer distorted the haze,
        But we needed, we needed, some rain.

As we pondered our fate, for our choices were few,
The horizon turned black as the thunderheads grew.
        And we stared, as we dared hope for rain.
As the storm gathered quickly with thunder and threat,
I felt joy well within me to see something wet,
        After so many months without rain.

Then it poured great big raindrops that bounced in the dirt,
But my dad didn't smile as it soaked through his shirt,
        And his tears were disguised by the rain.
Then he sighed in despair for the price we had paid,
"No, it won't even settle the dust, I'm afraid."
        For too little, too late, came the rain.

Dad's Working Years

After the war, Mom and Dad moved to Great Falls and set up shop as Modern Welding Service. Continuing his habit of adventuring, Dad collected another whole set of stories from his working years.

Johnny's 1952 Rocket 88

"I bought a brand new Oldsmobile,"
said Johnny Branch to Mitch,
"And now to pull a boat and such,
I need a trailer hitch."
Now Johnny was a welder,
and a pretty good one, too.
He'd mounted lots of hitches—
yes, he knew just what to do.

So one night after work when Mitch
and all the guys had gone,
He backed 'er in the shop to get
that trailer hitch put on.
He had to weld it to the frame,
a pretty simple deal,
So flipping down his helmet,
he touched welding rod to steel.

But then the fun began, as Johnny
swore through gritted teeth,
Because the arc he struck was on
the gas tank underneath!
He burned a little hole through which
the gas began to pour.
And horrified, he saw the fire
race across the floor.

The flames were headed toward the car,
the flowing fuel their guide.
So Johnny jumped behind the wheel
to pull the car outside.
The blaze was right behind him as
it followed out the door.
So trying to escape he pushed
the throttle to the floor.

His Rocket 88 shot forward,
        flaming from the rear.
He had to go, he couldn't slow,
        his plight was quite severe.
Attempting to outrun the blaze,
        avoiding traffic, too,
Around the block, across the bridge,
        what else was there to do?

But then he heard the siren
        as the fire truck appeared.
They doused the blaze, and with it
        all the horrors Johnny feared.
Though Johnny wouldn't talk,
        we all knew why he felt so dumb.
His car was blackened, and his tank
        was plugged with chewing gum!

The Wild Ride

We were hunting as usual, Johnny and I,
  On a typical clear autumn day.
With binoculars high on the top of a ridge
  We could scan a fair distance away.

Well we spotted some deer in the Blacktails below,
  And some bucks in among them, to boot.
They were just right across from our spot on the ridge,
  But we knew they were too far to shoot.

Now to get over there we would have to retrace
  Several miles, at least four or five.
We were driving my pickup, a '49 Chevy,
  Three-quarter ton two-wheel drive.

It was shorter, of course, if we headed straight down,
  And there weren't enough rocks there to mention.
The few scattered pines at the foot of the slope
  We could miss if we just paid attention.

Even sliding a little we'd probably make it
  On grass that was dusty and dry.
Having checked it out carefully, weighing the odds,
  We decided to give it a try.

Once committed we started to slide on the grass,
  And naturally then couldn't steer.
We would start to turn sideways and had to act quickly,
  Too busy to feel any fear.

I let up on the braking to straighten 'er out,
  But of course then we went even faster.
I'd brake and slide sideways and straighten again
  As I tried to avoid a disaster.

With our speed about fifty and trees coming quickly
    Our troubles had only begun.
So with minimum brakes and with maximum steer
    We went into the trees on the run.

Well, we flew through the trees about sixty or more,
    Only steering when touching the ground.
Then the slope leveled off and I managed to stop.
    We had come down the hill safe and sound.

We lost both of our mirrors and got some new scratches,
    But damage was not too severe.
And although I will always remember that ride,
    I forgot what became of those deer.

The Flood of '64

The Missouri was racing and raging,
Its floodwaters tossed with debris.
It was cloudy the night of high water,
So dark that a man couldn't see.
We were working two shifts at the shop,
And at midnight we quit for the night.
But before we all left I went down to the river
To see if our gear was alright.

The torrent was wild and rising,
Twelve inches or more every hour.
It was stealing some wooden concrete forms,
Like match sticks in all of that power.
So I got out all hands to the rescue,
And worked for an hour perhaps,
And we piled all the forms on the railroad embankment
Before going home to collapse.

After less than an hour of shut-eye,
The phone woke me up with a jerk.
It was Montana Power that called,
And they had some emergency work.
They said, "Black Eagle Dam is in danger!
There isn't a moment to lose!"
So I called out a couple of men from the dayshift.
It wasn't a job to refuse.

We put torches and tanks in the pickup,
And got to the dam about three.
It was blacker than ink with no power.
The lines had been downed by debris.
In the deafening roar of the torrent,
We yelled to be heard in the night.
And we rolled our equipment out onto the catwalk
While using a torch for a light.

What a scene was revealed in the torchlight!
The white water boiled against black.
With whole cottonwood trees piling up,
And the flood pouring through every crack.
The structure was shaking severely,
The river a battering ram,
And we held to the handrail as slowly we moved
Our equipment out onto the dam.

The support structure strained under pressure,
So flashboards could not be released.
And the catwalk, where trees lodged beneath it,
Was pulled down twelve inches at least.
So our job was to cut through the steel,
On the upriver side right below,
So the flashboards and trees, all the flooding debris,
And the surging Missouri could go.

I was first to lay flat on my belly,
A scene every man would repeat.
While the first man was holding the torchlight,
The other was holding my feet.
I reached down to cut the first I-beam,
The big eight inch beam under stress.
It took several cuts on the upriver side
And was hard on my nerves I confess.

When the beam finally broke and released,
Then the catwalk jumped up half a foot.
So while hanging down over the edge,
It was all I could do to stay put.
We considered a safety rope, too,
And could tie to the structure okay,
But nobody wanted to have on a rope
If the whole friggin' thing would give way.

By daylight we'd cut enough beams
So the stress on the structure was eased.
The flashboards would trip with a hammer,
And oh, were we tired—but pleased.
The Missouri was racing and raging,
Its floodwaters tossed with debris,
But the dam was secure and the danger was past,
For the flood was at last falling free.

Saga of Lindbergh Lake Capers

It was late in September, I clearly remember,
The first time we all got together.
And every year after, with drinks and with laughter,
We've gathered in all kinds of weather.

Now we all realize there are quite a few guys
That have come to the bashes we've held.
And the membership list contains two that are missed,
Ted Delaney and Bob Lichtenheld.

But we've added a few to the list of the crew,
Such as Ryan, and Stump from next door,
And Fitzgerald, and Meagher, and of course Kotschevar,
And Ukrainetz, and quite a few more.

Now we usually go with a dozen or so
Of the craziest guys on the block.
After twenty-five years, and through several careers,
It is probably time to take stock.

We prepare invitations with great dedication
And send them out yearly by letter.
Pretty soon it became quite an annual game
As the printing by Bennetts got better.

Now every edition confirmed our tradition
Of having a project or two.
And as they evolved, they became more involved
As the cabin expanded and grew.

Amid flora and fauna we dug out the sauna,
And one year the boathouse was built.
And we felled the big snag so the pickup could drag
The dead tree from its threatening tilt.

Now to top a dead tree was a challenge, you see,
Being too high to cut it or pull it.
So we hollered for Red, and we did what he said,
And we shot it and felled it with bullets.

While the others shoot trap, Uncle Frank takes a nap,
Whereas Goodover fishes for kicks.
With his saw and his gun, he can always have fun,
And then later they'll talk politics.

When we get in a panic and need a mechanic,
We holler for Louie or Red.
But they can't do it all, and the convoy last fall
Had two trucks that were towed out instead.

There's plenty to do for the chain sawing crew,
As the orange monster splits the logs thinner.
There's boating and fishing and skiing and wishing
We hadn't had so much for dinner.

Only two meals a day, but the food is gourmet,
What with three gourmet cooks all in charge.
Although fighting the bulge, we do overindulge,
As our repasts become rather large.

Now when Homer cooks dinner, it's always a winner.
And Bersch fixes excellent fare.
And our Saturday night is a gourmet's delight
When we sample what Kotch can prepare.

While the rest of us ache, then Doc Hulett and Jake
Will do dishes, and proud of it, too.
And Bailey will look at his new girlie book,
And Rivera plays rummy on cue.

Now Ukrainetz and Ryan are not really tryin'
To make sure they'll always be here.
So we added two more to the men of our corps,
To our own Rod of Aaron last year.

So now Stephens is new, and Al Kolstad is, too.
We hope each will be one of the guys.
We can play pretty hard, as we let down our guard,
Reminisce, and tell stories and lies.

Now we used to raise cain and be feeling no pain
And the neighborhood thought us deranged.
But lately our capers don't bother the neighbors,
And oh, how the tempo has changed!

Now Bennetts, for instance, no more goes the distance,
And drinks Diet Coke like it's free.
And the booze cost is not in the number-one slot,
But has fallen to slot number three.

Whereas Frisbee would choose select wine as his booze,
Now just any old Boone's Farm will serve.
And old Whetstone no more will eat shrimp by the score
Or a salmon just as an hors d'oeuvre.

I remember the boys used to like to make noise,
And would hit Liquid Louie's by ten.
But lately instead they would all go to bed
Like a bunch of contented old men.

But we still blunder through what we come here to do,
To recharge, get our vigor restored.
So relax, get away, and have fun when you stay
With yours truly, old bald eagle Ward.

My Private Years

Each poem drawn from my own life exposes a little bit more about me, my fears, my joys, and the events that helped to shape my life. When I was growing up, I unabashedly wrote little poems of my innocent experiences, my simple feelings, and my developing perceptions of life.

As an adult, however, until recently, I would not have risked unmasking the real me. My poems were few and far between and did not violate my privacy. I wrote of my horses and my dogs in those years, and other people's adventures.

Somewhere along the line I learned to laugh at myself, just a little bit. What a joy and a relief to finally begin to allow others in on some of my secrets. I don't know why it never occurred to me before that other people have night monsters, too.

Tale of the Kittiwake

There are many tales of seas and sails
That seamen will relate.
And the more they're told, they become more bold
As seamen exaggerate.

But I have a tale of the sea and of sail
That is true as the gospel, I swear.
Though I was a landman instead of a seaman,
It happened to me. I was there.

It was early in May on the Chesapeake Bay,
I had offered to help out a friend.
He decided to take his old yawl, Kittiwake,
Where the leak in her hull he could mend.

We started with three, the young captain and me,
And another young man as first mate.
We collected our gear, I provided the beer,
And we boarded one Friday night, late.

We intended to stay there until the next day
And then leisurely head for the Bay.
But with radio warning of storm before morning,
We decided to get underway.

We would make our way south to a place past the mouth
Of the mile-wide Potomac by noon.
We intended to sail way ahead of the gale.
We just didn't expect it so soon.

The first mate, it was clear, had had way too much beer,
For he went below deck about then.
He was wrapped 'round the table as best he was able,
And we never did see him again.

After midnight we entered the channel that's centered
For ships to and from Baltimore.
We kept taking in sail with the force of the gale,
And the noise became nearly a roar.

My friend was the one with the knowledge to run
To the bow, to the lines, to the mast.
"Tack into the wind!" he would shout as he grinned.
"Man the tiller! Make everything fast!"

In the great sheets of rain it was hard to remain
On the deck being tossed by the sea.
And I feared if he fell overboard on a swell
Then the only one left would be me.

We were fighting the storm, working hard to keep warm,
As the long night became cold and dreary.
And out of the gloom silent freighters would loom,
And we both became fearful and weary.

It was getting toward dawn, yet the tempest wore on.
So our night surely hadn't been dull!
And our craft was too long, for the waves hit her wrong
And incessantly pounded her hull.

When I went below deck, just to make a quick check,
I saw water slosh up from the floor.
What had been a small leak in a seam that was weak
Was a hole of four inches or more.

The pump we had going was not even slowing
Our water intake, I could see.
So we added a pump from the engine to dump
Yet more water back into the sea.

But we still were not gaining with both our pumps straining,
So I had to start pumping by hand.
And as we succeeded, the water receded.
There still was a chance to reach land.

Then my friend patched the leak, but I knew it was weak.
Oh, that cotton he used seemed so thin!
I wanted to hail the next freighter to bail
Ourselves out of the fix we were in.

But my friend was quite sure of the strength of his cure,
And we crossed the Potomac okay.
We ran nearly aground in the harbor we found,
But decided to stay anyway.

I was tired and relieved but I finally believed
What those seamen had been telling me.
Now I am a seaman instead of a landman
And this is my tale of the sea.

There are many tales of seas and sails
That seamen will relate.
And the more they're told, they become more bold
As seamen exaggerate.

MIDNIGHT

I was thirty years old when I got my first horse,
And what happened was none of my doing, of course.
I was greener than grass in a pasture in spring,
And, I'm sorry to say, didn't know anything.

On one Saturday night I was having a beer
In a bar down in Three Forks, a ways west of here.
I was saying to Pete, and to Stacy, his wife,
That I'd wanted a horse of my own all my life.

Now, old Pete was a rancher who lived around there,
And a horseman, to boot, who would trade fair and square.
So I toasted his health and I asked if someday
He would help me to buy a good horse for my pay.

So he said that he would, and I promptly forgot,
Because over a beer a guy says quite a lot.
But on Monday he called, without any remorse,
And said, "Hi, this is Pete. I just bought you a horse!"

Well, I couldn't renege, so I said that was great,
But I started to wonder how much horses ate.
With a two acre place and no barn and no fence,
The idea of having a horse made no sense.

Now the horse had been on winter pasture since fall
And he never had seen the inside of a stall.
He was born on a ranch and had lived there for years
As a pony for ropin' and cuttin' the steers.

So on Tuesday Pete trailered the horse to his place,
And he rode him and calmed him and petted his face.
Then he picked out a bridle, right from his own tack,
And he bought a used saddle and pad for his back.

There were only four days to find someplace to board,
And I hoped that I'd find one that I could afford.
But a friend offered his place for six weeks for free,
So it all fell in place with no effort from me.

I began to distrust what I thought I had heard,
But on Friday old Pete was as good as his word.
It had rained all day long and the pastures were wet,
And was getting toward dark when we finally met.

I jumped out of the car and ran over to see
Just what manner of horse he had chosen for me.
He was taller than most of the horses I'd seen,
And his coat was pure black, and he looked strong and lean.

As I made his acquaintance, Pete watched with a grin.
"His name's Midnight," he said. "Wanna go for a spin?"
So I led him to where I could get on his back,
For I needed a fence, or a little haystack.

Then I went for a ride, and at once I could tell
That once I learned to ride, we would get along well.
Now it's been several years since that very first ride,
And I still have old Midnight, a source of great pride.

Lady Got Lost

It was during the summer that Lady got lost.
But it wasn't her fault; she had been double-crossed.
She was still pretty young, just a year or two old,
And she tried very hard to do all she was told.

But Puppy was older and it was agreed
That Lady would follow where Puppy would lead.
One weekend we went to my folks' for a visit,
The location of which for a dog is exquisite.

With mountains and bushes and mice and brown rabbits,
And deer running loose with such chaseable habits.
On Saturday morning the dogs went outside
For their "morning relief," Puppy said, but she lied.

By noon or before, we had started to doubt her,
And then the next day, Puppy came home without her.
She pranced around saucily—made no pretention.
Puppy hadn't got lost, she had paid more attention.

But Lady was lost, there could be no mistake.
With no food and no hugs, there was too much at stake.
So Puppy and Steve spent the rest of the day
Hiking miles of ridges in search of our stray.

And they asked at the house up the creek just in case,
But no Lady, no luck. Just a wild goose chase.
So at last we gave up and went home Sunday night
With the hope that our dog would somehow be alright.

But on Monday the neighbor who lived up the creek
Called to say that a dog (who had talked a blue streak)
Had appeared at his door with her tale of woe,
And he thought that perhaps we'd be wanting to know.

So Dad went to get her, and learned where she'd been,
For she started her story all over again.
In two days she had gone fifty miles or more
And her footpads were ragged, and boy, were they sore!

She was tired and lonely—"Where is everyone?"
She was worried and hungry, but still she'd had fun.
She babbled incessantly all the way home,
And she promised that never again would she roam.

When they got to the house and she learned we had gone,
She worried a little, then gave a big yawn.
Then she laid herself down on the carpeted floor,
And she slept like a log for six hours or more.

There is more to the story, and I could expound,
But the point is that Lady was home safe and sound.
We thought she was cured, and no more would she venture,
But Puppy had plans for another adventure!

Escape

It was one of those days when your wandering gaze
Is bedazzled by skies that are fair.
And it still was midwinter, and sharp were the splinters
Of ice that still hung in the air.

Now a couple of dogs had been sleeping like logs
Every day in their pen and were bored.
It was time to escape and get into a scrape
So their interest in life is restored.

So Lady was guided when Puppy decided
To climb the dog pen at the gate.
It was such a nice morning, and there was no warning
Of weather to alter their fate.

So with two wagging tails, they went up to the trails
That went into the forest unknown.
At that time of the year there were rabbits and deer,
And they sniffed every bush and each stone.

All the birds were in song as they trotted along,
When it suddenly started to storm.
Since they'd started to roam, they were miles from home,
So they hid under trees to stay warm.

The temperature dropped and the snow never stopped
As it piled up deeper and deeper.
And it muffled the sound as it built up around
The big tree, and the sides became steeper.

They were trapped in the well by the snow as it fell,
And they couldn't escape for two days.
They had nothing to eat and there wasn't much heat,
Though they promised to alter their ways.

With their final appeal came a lone snowmobile,
And the man saw the dogs and their plight.
He was tempted to shoot, but they both were so cute,
And they hailed him with honest delight.

He decided to give them a chance to still live,
So he broke a rough trail to the tree.
With no choice but to leap through the snow four feet deep
They came bounding out, glad to be free.

To go home was to go back uphill through the snow,
And this time they were not playing games.
But their luck was still good, and from out of the wood
They could hear someone calling their names.

It was Steve on his skis bringing sausage and cheese
To the rescue without much delay.
Their reunion was cheerful, if not downright tearful.
A miracle happened that day.

A Chink in the Armor

Emerging from my cocoon of insecurity, I feel the freedom of the butterfly!

Wind and the Night Monsters

Late at night I hear the wind, as sleep is so elusive,
Howling so relentlessly, its pounding so abusive.
Gusting anger, making all the bushes bow before it,
Never even tempo, making sure I can't ignore it.

Fearful thoughts can dominate, distort my normal thinking,
Making all my problems worse—my sanity is shrinking.
Panic now attacks and Worry offers its assistance.
Helpless as the bushes, I can muster no resistance.

Logic drives my mind to work, but logic isn't working.
Constant interrupting by the fears that still are lurking.
Mournfully the tempest wails as fitfully I fight it,
Wide awake exhausted, yet I must have slept despite it.

Puppy kisses warm my nose and wake me without warning,
Cheerful wagging innocence, she greets me in the morning.
Daylight muffles howling wind and dissipates my worries.
Blizzard night conditions fade to merely scattered flurries.

SECRETS

I have noticed that most of the people will boast,
When they speak of the source of their pride.
I suspect that a few of the people who do
Also have a few secrets to hide.

To that simple perception I find no exception
Upon introspection of me.
But I really prefer to adroitly refer
To my right to have some privacy.

I would rather not talk of the hole in my sock,
Or the pimple that's right where I sit.
Or a couple of habits that increased like rabbits,
So now it is harder to quit.

And I, too, pick my nose, and then wipe on my clothes.
Now come on! What do you do with yours?
Do you eat it? Or drip it? Or roll it and flip it?
How much of it lands on our floors?

And what about gases that everyone passes?
The air that we breathe must be rank!
But with hemorrhoids or piles, you can hear it for miles.
Excuse me for being so frank.

When I feel like a belch that I really should squelch,
Then I swallow and keep my mouth closed.
Because Heaven forbid if you see what I did,
'Cause that's tacky—or so I've supposed.

And I frankly consider it most inconsiderate,
Scratching yourself where it itches.
Unless it's instead on your arm or your head,
Or it's one of those crazy skin twitches.

Now why am I shy, as my actions belie
What are everyday bodily functions?
I should be deciding to come out of hiding.
I shouldn't have any compunctions.

I have sins of omission as well as commission,
Like vacuuming under the bed.
And when no one is there, then I really don't care,
And I watch television instead.

When it comes to my cooking, when nobody's looking,
I'll slurp it right out of the pan.
Although toothpicks are dandy, my fingernail's handy.
I'm crude as Neanderthal Man!

But my self-condemnation for procrastination
Has never affected a cure.
And my new-found obsession for secret confession
Has not made me any more pure!

Ode to Wind

I can't believe the crazy wind,
it's driving people nuts.
Just opening the door to leave
can take a lot of guts.
I think I've made it through, and then
it slams me in the face.
Why, even doors inside the house—
it's windy everyplace.

It howls in all the crevices
where windows don't quite fit.
It rattles in the chimney like
it's never going to quit.
It gurgles in the darn commode
and sucks the water down.
It carries asphalt shingles to the
other side of town.

The other day the winds derailed
a train just west of here,
And semi-trucks blow off the road—
it makes it hard to steer.
With gusts approaching eighty, and
no sign that it would cease,
McWind destroyed the golden arches,
piece by golden piece.

One fearsome gust destroys a windmill,
wrecks a weather vane,
So now we measure wind by how
it blows a logging chain.
At first I said I didn't mind,
and actually I meant it.
But after weeks of battering,
I'm starting to resent it.

I feel like hitting back when it
        attacks my battered door,
But spitting in the wind just doesn't
        even up the score.
This morning it was quiet!
        I was so surprised, I grinned!
But on the morning news report,
        the forecast calls for . . . wind!

REVENUE

A ways beyond McAllister,
        and past North Meadow Creek,
Upon the high plateau, before
        the trees get very thick,

Where only sage can grow against
        the raw November wind,
And Mother Nature punishes
        the weak for having sinned,

The mining camp of Revenue
        is fading from the land,
A ghost of what it used to be,
        one building left to stand.

A one-room shack, once strong and proud,
        and sturdy as the rock,
Now leaning, bowing to defeat—
        if only it could talk.

The huge equipment, still in place,
        its iron rusted red,
Can testify to shattered dreams,
        to visions long since dead.

The gold that lured those hopeful men
        is lying there in wait
To tempt the modern miner
        to the same relentless fate.

But Mother Nature offers other
        riches of the earth
Whose value isn't measured in
        their monetary worth.

I lean against a rock to just
        absorb the beauty here,
A beauty raw and rugged
        that will never disappear.

It never changes, always changes,
        never quite the same,
This bleak and unforgiving land
        that man can never tame.

I feel the peace of centuries,
        as worries fall away.
The stillness permeates my soul—
        I learned to live today.

The Revenue is not the gold,
        elusive as it seems.
The priceless gift this country gives
        is peace beyond our dreams.

Cold Fear

Setting now, the winter sun removes its feeble warming.
Rapidly the darkness spreads its cold with wind and storming.
Fear invades my soul, a fear that's cold and penetrating,
Growing exponentially with every hour of waiting.

Futilely my walls withstand the cold as it advances.
Fear destroys my confidence in taking any chances.
Howling wind finds every crack and breathes its icy hisses,
Frosting doors and windowsills where weather stripping misses.

Worry escalates to panic, tunnel vision thinking,
Spiral-feeding on itself, inexorably sinking.
Logical assurances, or words of comfort chosen,
Nothing now can calm my nerves, my mind is panic-frozen.

Totally exhausted from the focus of my worry,
Wanting to be done with it, I wish the end would hurry.
Bravely I approach my fear to see what it is made of.
What exactly is the problem I am so afraid of?

Happiness is what's at stake! Its loss must be prevented.
How can I ignore the possibilities presented?
What if all the worst would happen? What if it were real?
How the pain would rack my soul! I know how it would feel.

Suddenly the waiting ends. The grip of fear releases,
Breaking solid ice into a thousand little pieces.
Sunshine feels so wonderful! My brain is finally clearing.
Life again is liveable, with worry disappearing.

UNCONDITIONAL LOVE

She is beautiful there, with the sun through her hair,
In a halo of soft morning light.
And her temples are smooth as I touch her to soothe
And assure her that things are all right.

Then her eyebrows will rise over melting big eyes
As she tells me she tries to be good.
And her joy will abound as she dances around.
She would turn inside out if she could.

She is true to her feelings in all of her dealings,
And couldn't deceive if she tried.
And I often reflect at how much I respect
Total honesty, free of false pride.

If I ask her to wait for the steak on her plate,
She will drool with the charm of a 'gator.
With her heart and her soul she will swallow it whole,
And will fart in the living room later.

There is never a doubt what she's thinking about,
By her eyes or the smile on her face,
Or the cock of her ear, or her tail in gear
Wagging circles all over the place.

And wherever I go, she is close by, I know,
For she never gets too far apart.
And whatever my fear, she will always be near,
Unconditional love in her heart.

Deserted

The aging house stands empty now,
Its homey feeling gone somehow.
    The windmill standing silently for years.
The pair of cottonwoods has grown,
Providing shade, though all alone
    Where someone left behind their dreams and tears.

I wonder what they did for fun,
And what became of everyone,
    And how it would have been if they had stayed.
But even though the folks have gone,
The cows still gather on the lawn
    To spend some summer hours in the shade.

Things That Remind Me of Mom

A meadowlark fluting his cheeriest trill,
Or some sweet peas and crocuses soft on the hill,
Or a dish full of pansies, bright colored and gay,
Just a few in some water, so pretty that way.

Or the scent of fresh air in clean sheets that were dried
By the breeze in the sun on the clothesline outside.
Or a brisk walk at dawn, or a fresh loaf of bread,
Or at night just a small glass of milk before bed.

Every time when I visit and time comes to leave,
I'm reminded how she'd rather give than receive.
A few slices of roast for my dinner that night,
Or some "leftover" goulash that turned out just right.

Or a story she found that she wanted to share,
Or a beautiful coat that she "just doesn't wear".
Or a picture of me as a cute little tyke
That she just ran across and thought maybe I'd like.

Or, "Today with the raspberries all coming on,
You should take some, or next time you come they'll be gone."
Or some tiny young carrots, and fresh spinach, too,
And green onions and garlic, just extra she grew.

Simple deeds that are done without fanfare or fame,
Without thought of reward, but with love just the same.
Little things become more with the warmth of her touch,
And remind me I love her, I love her so much.

LITTLE PLEASURES IN LIFE

The midday sun was hot and dry,
As usual in late July,
        No shade at all, and chance of rain was bleak.
But three old cows had common sense,
For where they gathered by the fence
        The irrigation pipe had sprung a leak!

The arcing spray was full and wet,
And smelled like springtime rain, I bet.
        And rainbow crystals hung there all the while.
The pipe ran four feet off the ground,
So those three cows just stood around,
        And in their drenching rain I saw them smile!

Flight and the Daily Doldrums

Daily life can get distorted, thoughts become defective.
Going places far away can change my whole perspective.
Living in a fog and needing something to remind me,
Lifting off the runway, leaving everything behind me.

Tiny buildings vanishing and Planet Earth appearing,
Problems that I thought were looming, now are disappearing.
Fear and Worry lose their grip, my thoughts become more pleasant.
Slipping through the veil of clouds, I focus on the present.

Now in level flight and feeling noticeably lighter,
Floating high, my mind expanding, feeling ever brighter.
Something new to think about, of people and of places,
Empathizing, tuning in to other people's spaces.

Flying home, at peace within, no turbulent emotion,
Sky and clouds are everywhere, with no apparent motion.
Stronger now, and more aware, and wanting to be doing,
Dropping boldly into clouds, within the storm that's brewing.

The Fourth of July

'Twas the Fourth of July and their spirits were high
As the townspeople gathered together.
The fireworks display would go on anyway,
In spite of the threatening weather.

They had come to the park and were waiting for dark,
For the blackening backdrop of night.
They had all paid the fee and were anxious to see
The magnificent colorful sight.

The big mortars had bore of eight inches or more,
And their aerial bombs were the best.
Then the remnants of day slipped away, slipped away,
And the thunderheads grew in the west.

When the fireworks began, electricity ran
Through the crowd like a frenzy through sharks.
Then the mortars reloaded and more bursts exploded
In showers of colorful sparks.

What a glorious show! All their faces aglow!
It was perfect, with never a snag.
And the rocket's red glare, the bombs bursting in air,
Made their hearts swell with pride for their flag.

Then the storm struck at last with a bright lightning blast,
Silhouetting the mountains like dawn.
As the crowd hushed in wonder, the crack of the thunder
Rolled echoing rumbling on.

As the storm gathered fury, the show had to hurry
To finish before drenching rain.
But each colorful shower got lost in that power.
The efforts of man were in vain.

Each person would wonder why God stole their thunder.
He certainly won it that day.
Or perhaps He supports Independence Day sports,
And was joining the fun in His way!

The Dance of the Doe

As the dawn poked its way through the meadow's tall grass,
And the dew beaded up on each blade,
Not a breath broke the silence, the river like glass,
And two does sniffed the air from the shade.

Then they cautiously ventured out into the sun,
Followed closely by three tiny fawns.
Reddish tan with white spots and too spindly to run,
They must hide while the does carry on.

In the deep tangled grass where the fawns made their beds,
They instinctively knew they must stay
Without moving at all, their ears flat to their heads,
While the does grazed the hours away.

In the lengthening shadows as evening drew near,
The first doe found her twins right away.
But the other doe searched with a heightening fear
That her fawn may have wandered astray.

In a panic with dread, but refusing to yield,
She methodically started the hunt.
From the creek in the corner she worked the whole field,
Nose to ground from the back to the front.

After minutes like hours, her nose touched his hair,
And her heart gave a tentative leap.
He was perfectly motionless, camouflaged there,
Where the grass was so tangled and deep.

When she nuzzled him gently he got up at last,
A bit wobbly but ready to go.
And no human emotion has ever surpassed
All the joy in the dance of that doe!

About the Poet

A glance around Carol Hample's small suburban home in Bozeman, Montana, verifies her preference for simplicity. "I try to cut through to the essence," she explains, "in my daily schedule, in my surroundings, and in my writings. Clutter is not required."

A stickler for precision, and a longtime fan of the rhythmic poetry of Robert Service and Edgar Allen Poe, Carol began as a little girl to hone her skills in the art of rhythm and rhyme. Combining her flair for precision and simplicity, she needed only the tale to be told.

Drawing from her own experiences, she wrote heartwarming poems and rollicking sagas. Needing more subject matter, she turned to her father, a teller of tales from his own store of experiences growing up in Montana in the 1920s and 1930s. His way of laughing at himself, and of making light of what others may consider misadventures, all told in his unique staccato manner, provided material that meshed perfectly with her own developing poetic style.

Carol's poetry has appeared in several publications, and she participates in various poetry gatherings. In 1988 she was the first recipient of the Golden Star Award for Poetry.

Born in 1947 in Great Falls to Albert B. "Red" and Madge H. Dismore, Carol has lived nearly all her life in Montana. She and her sister Linda grew up as best friends on the outskirts of town. "We rode our bikes everywhere, played with polliwogs in mud puddles, and climbed on houses under construction, even though we weren't supposed to," she remembers. After receiving a Master of Science degree in mathematics from Montana State University, she moved to Maryland for three years, gaining new experiences and changing careers. Returning to Bozeman in 1978 as a new CPA, she now lives with her dog Lady.